BRITAIN IN OLD PH...

ALONG THE
THAMES

BRIAN EADE

SUTTON PUBLISHING LIMITED

Sutton Publishing Limited
Phoenix Mill · Thrupp · Stroud
Gloucestershire · GL5 2BU

First published 1997
Reprinted 1999

Cover photographs: *front*: Lock-keeper James
Bossom and his wife at Clifton lock, *c.* 1898;
back: Amy Kirby towing her dog, Penton Hook
lock.
Title page: Author and father, Clifton Hampden,
1959

British Library Cataloguing in Publication Data
A catalogue record for this book is available from
the British Library.

ISBN 0-7509-1543-9

Typeset in 10/12 Perpetua.
Typesetting and origination by
Sutton Publishing Limited.
Printed in Great Britain by
Redwood Books, Trowbridge, Wiltshire.

This book is dedicated to my late parents, Vivien and Eric Eade.

CONTENTS

The overgrown lock chamber at Inglesham in the summer of 1968 marks the entrance to the abandoned Thames & Severn canal, opened in 1789 and costing in the region of £200,000 to build. It finally closed in 1927, although many volunteers are working hard for its re-opening. Behind the lock is the distinctive Roundhouse that once housed the lock-keeper or watchman in very limited accommodation. The ground floor was devoted to stabling with a living-room on the second floor and a bedroom on the third floor. Five of these unusual roundhouses were built on this canal at Cerney Wick, Chalford, Coates, Inglesham and Marston Meysey.

INTRODUCTION

The Thames is not just a great river. It is also a vital watercourse for transporting goods and people. Exploitation of the river for these purposes spans the centuries, during which many man-made changes to its course and flow have improved navigation. In particular, locks have improved travel along the Thames and the lock-keepers are the largely unsung heroes of the river. This book presents a picture of their life and work along the Thames, from its head to Richmond.

'Once he was asked, what, in his heart of hearts he most wanted to be? After some thought, Ian replied that his true ambition was to be a lock-keeper on the River Thames. "There I would stand amongst my phloxes and snapdragons and watch life go by in an orderly manner"' (*The Flame Trees of Thika*). For the majority of people that is probably how the life of a lock-keeper is seen. For many, a lock is a pleasant place to visit on a sunny afternoon to watch the boats go through. Looking after all of this is the lock-keeper, directing operations and ensuring the safe running of the lock. When a problem arises, the lock-keeper is the first person to turn to. There can be many problems to deal with during the course of a year, with people and animals falling in, boat fires, injuries, rescues and recovering bodies. On some occasions the lock-keeper has to be a fine judge of the human character, defusing tempers and turning potential arguments into acceptable compromises.

What are locks and why are they there? Some lock-keepers jokingly reply, 'to annoy the boaters!' However, the lock evolved from an early method of controlling water: the 'flash weir'. Years ago, the Thames had few weirs to regulate its flow and floods were commonplace. Weirs were introduced to control the flow and alleviate flooding. There were also millers, monks, fishermen and barge operators who had a vested interest in maintaining water levels. Later, these weirs developed into locks, not in the modern sense, but more of a dam with removable parts to allow craft literally to 'flash' down on the released rush of water. Going upstream was more laborious, with the craft having to be winched or towed up against the current. This method was quite wasteful and resulted in long delays while the water built up again.

Clearly a better method was required, and the 'pound' lock was developed. A much cruder version than we see today, it often had turf walls, but the principle remained the same – water held in a 'pound' with gates at each end and sluices allowing water to enter and leave the lock. The locks on the Thames are perhaps best described as a water staircase, with each lock as a step, going up or down the river.

More weirs were built over the years, and flash weirs were converted to pound locks. This whole process was changed and revised countless times to provide the system we see today. An outstanding relic of these early times is the pound lock in Swift Ditch near Abingdon. Built by the Thames Commissioners over 350 years ago, it remains largely intact and worthy of better husbandry.

Throughout all these changes, one fact remained constant – the person looking after the lock and weir. The position of lock-keeper evolved like the locks themselves. Sometimes he was the landlord of a local pub, or perhaps a fishing-weir owner who also collected tolls. Either way, it was often required that the lock-keeper looked after more than one lock and weir at a time and sometimes a ferry as well.

The most important aspect of lock-keeping is monitoring and maintaining water levels, which are read several times a day from gauges at the top (head) and bottom (tail) of the lock. Depending on the movement up or down of the river, the keeper will make the necessary adjustments on the weir. Each weir is different and its peculiarities have to be learnt by a process known as 'trial and terror'. Make a mistake, and the results are there for all to see. Forget important safety precautions and the keeper may pay dearly. During summer the flow on the Thames is minimal, with riverside vegetation taking up moisture and losses from evaporation. During this time the weirs are usually closed to maintain the level of water in the reach between locks. In the other seasons the opposite is true: high rainfall, waterlogged ground and run-off from land drainage. On these occasions the weir may be said to be 'fully drawn', that is, all available tackle is out and the water thunders through. The lock-keeper can do little else on the weir, but be ready to act quickly in case a 'slump' strikes. This could occur overnight, as rain stops and the water rushes away downstream. In extreme cases, the reach could be drained of water by morning!

What are the realities of life as a lock-keeper? Much easier than they were a few years ago. As recently as 1964 some of the locks were without electricity, and remote locks may still be cut off for weeks in harsh winters, either by floods or by snow. The working hours are much improved. Gone are the days of working 7.30 a.m. to sunset (which could be as late as 10.20 p.m. in double summertime). All that work, and then only one day off to recover! An improvement on 1903, when leave was 'allowed 7 days annually on full pay, and they may have a further 7 days at intervals if they desire, provided that such leave involves no cost to the Conservators'.

Lock-keepers occasionally act as water bailiffs, mainly checking that anglers have valid rod licences. As water bailiffs, they have similar authority to that of a police constable and may 'examine any dam, fishing weir, fishing mill dam, fixed engine or obstruction, or any artificial watercourse, and for that purpose enter on any land'. Also they may 'stop and search any boat or other vessel used in fishing'. All of these powers and more are subject to the phrase 'reasonable cause to suspect'. Watch out! There's a bailiff about.

The pace of the lock-keeper's life ebbs and flows with the seasons, each time of year bringing its own tasks and events. What do lock-keepers do in the winter? While there may be fewer boats to let through the work never stops. Weir work and clearance, painting, garden preparation, lock scrubbing, inventory and countless other jobs are left over from the rest of the year.

After the long, hard slog of winter, comes the boating season proper, although there are those who like to cruise regardless of the time of year or the condition of the river. Even experienced boaters may still be caught out by sudden increases of water level and find themselves in difficulty. However, over the years, Easter has been seen as the traditional start to the boating season and a time of dread for lock-keepers. Poorly maintained boats out for the first time after a winter lay-off have a tendency to fail at the most inappropriate times and the first of the season's hire boats venture out with inexperienced crews, giving the lock-keeper lots to watch out for, especially if the weather is inclement. These boats often do not have licences valid for the new season, causing mountains of extra paperwork.

Once the weather improves, so the volume of river traffic increases and the lock-keeper is kept very busy. However, reward often comes in the form of cold liquid refreshment dispensed by the boaters and generally the great British public that infest the lock sides during summer are in a happy and genial frame of mind. As autumn blows in, bringing rain, floods, rubbish and frequent demands to visit the weir, the lock-keeper begins to look forward to quieter times when the emphasis is on water control.

As each year unfolds, the lock-keeper seldom has time to consider how others may view, with some envy perhaps, the variety, diversity and quality of the lock-keeper's life besides the ever-changing Thames.

ABOVE OXFORD

The stretch above Oxford is arguably the most tranquil stretch of the Thames, with the extremely low Osney bridge preventing larger vessels from progressing any further. There have been many improvements to navigation over the years, including the construction of six new pound locks between the years 1771 and 1811, and the removal of some obstructions. The Thames & Severn canal opened in 1790 joining the Thames above Lechlade, thereby increasing barge traffic. Difficulties remained with the dilapidated remnants of flash weirs left in place by local landowners; eventually the power to take over most of these structures was sanctioned by an act of Parliament (Thames Navigation Act 1866). After negotiating with interested parties and raising the required revenue from six London water companies, dredging and other works were undertaken to prevent flooding in the Oxford locality. By 1924 the Thames Conservancy's policy of improvement had turned to the remaining flash weirs at Eaton Hastings, Eynsham, Kings and Medley. These old structures were removed by 1928, with new pound locks and weirs being built at Eynsham and Kings. The flash weirs at Eaton Hastings and Medley were last used in about 1937, and dismantled shortly after.

Thames head near Cricklade, early October 1958. Acknowledged by most as the real source of the Thames, it is now probably a dried-up hollow. The statue of old Father Thames, which used to watch over the source, was relocated to the lockside at St John's in the early 1970s to prevent further attacks from vandals.

The last full immersion Thames baptism at Cricklade, probably *c.* 1900. Little more is known except that the ceremony was probably performed just above a bridge known as Plank Bridge. It appears to have been quite an event – more than one hundred people were present including babes in arms.

St John's lock in 1864, from the towpath bank, with probably the first lock cottage situated on the island. Clearly, regular maintenance was not top priority judging by the amount of water gushing through the rotten lock gates. The spire of Lechlade church can be seen in the distance.

The Thames Conservancy's steam launch, *Donola*, in St John's lock on annual inspection in the 1960s, with the Inspector, Mr Stapleton, on the lockside. In the background on the lock island is the wooden lock office.

The huge distillery on Brandy island with Buscot lock in the foreground, *c.* 1870. Costing almost £100,000 to build and equip, the distillery formed part of local gentleman Robert Campbell's 'great agricultural experiment', namely intensive farming. From sugar beet, sugar and spirit were extracted and then despatched in casks to France for use in making brandy. There were other works on the island, including gasworks, a mill, vitriol works and facilities for manufacturing artificial fertilizer. Thames Water currently has an intake on the site of the distillery.

Thames Conservancy launch *Seven Springs* in Buscot lock, *c.* 1960. In the open fields behind the lock a second weir was built, unusual in that it was constructed first and connected to the main river later.

The original weir at Buscot in 1910, still in use today but without the original paddles and rymers. A second weir was built in 1979 on the other side of the lock. The cottage to the left of the weir is now in National Trust ownership, but at one time housed the relief lock-keeper until a new property was built in 1971, when a full-time keeper was appointed. The undershot waterwheel was one of several installed in the area by Robert Campbell to pump water via cast iron pipes to a reservoir on his estate, providing the irrigation required for his intensive farming methods.

The waterwheel at Buscot on its last day of service, 11 April 1935. A traction engine has already been connected by a belt to drive the water pump. The 3.6 m diameter wheel ran between 4 and 5 rpm producing approximately 21 horsepower. Nearly 5 m wide, all that is visible today are the wear marks scored into the wall of the brickwork channel.

Snowdrift going upstream through Eaton Hastings or Hart's weir, 1930. The forerunner of a pound lock, the 'flash' weir was simply a dam with removable parts. The parts of this type of weir were rymers and paddles. The rymer was a variable length of wood (dependent on the depth of weir) about 100 mm square with a tee handle. The paddles were round poles with boards fixed across at the base. They had offset handles to allow a number of paddles to be put in, usually three, bottom, middle and top (known as a set). Pitching rymers was a tricky operation, with one foot on the weir platform and the other on the beam that held the rymers in position. Then, as the term suggests, the rymer was 'pitched' upstream and pushed down through the water to locate on the base. If the base was missed first time the rymer was dropped or the inevitable resulted! Dropped rymers were collected later from the weir pool in the lock boat, or occasionally they ended up at the next lock down. Once two rymers were in place, then the paddles could be slid down in the correct order to the bottom. On deep weirs the paddles had to be hammered down with a wooden mallet. With one 'set' in, the other rymers were 'walked' along in front of the set to their position on the base. This all appears to be fairly straightforward, especially on a clear dry day. Not quite so easy on a wet winter's day in blustery winds, when this type of work was usually required.

The Anchor Inn at Eaton Hastings flash weir, 1910. Neither the inn nor the weir survives. The inn was destroyed by fire in the winter of 1979/80, with the tragic loss of three lives. The weir, one of the last of its kind in operation, was not removed until 1937, along with Medley weir, near Oxford.

Snowdrift passing down through Eaton Hastings weir on a 'flash' of released water, 1930.

Grafton lock, one of the most remote lock-houses on the river in the 1950s, it finally had electricity installed in the early 1960s. With the river in flood, the lock-keeper had to row the lock dinghy to the nearest road. In severe winters, the lock could be completely cut off with the added burden of a frozen water supply. One lock-keeper's wife nearly paid with her life fetching water from the frozen lock. She slipped and fell on to ice in the lock and laid there unconscious for several hours. Returning later, her husband searched frantically for her, eventually discovering her in the frozen lock. Rushed to hospital for emergency treatment, she was extremely fortunate to survive her ordeal.

The bridge over the 'new' cut at Radcot, c. 1910. The cut was excavated in 1787 to accommodate the extra traffic expected from the Thames and Severn canal. The wooden footbridge crosses a backwater leading to one of the former wharves. Many tons of stone were shipped by barge from these wharves to rebuild London after the Great Fire. In front of the arch can be seen a great deal of vegetation typical of the upper reaches at that time. The Swan Inn is in the background.

Said to be the oldest surviving Thames bridge, the original navigation bridge at Radcot, photographed from the Berkshire bank, *c.* 1910. The two outer arches date from *c.* 1200, but the rounded centre arch is more recent, *c.* 1395. On the downstream parapet niche there once rested a statue of the Virgin Mary, which was destroyed during the Civil War. The metal-skinned canoe in the foreground is from the Swan Inn's hire fleet.

An unusual photograph of a weed elevator, which as the name suggests was used to carry weed up out of the river. It is not known whether the weed was used as feed or fertilizer, but judging by the stack being created it obviously had a use.

Radcot lock and old house looking downstream, 1954: a quiet and isolated lock, with the nearest houses a mile away. This lock was occasionally used as a spell in 'solitary' for lock-keepers who had misbehaved elsewhere. In July of that year the peace of the night was shattered by a tremendous explosion close to the lock-house. A B47 bomber, from the 51st Squadron, Fairford, had crashed close to Old Man's footbridge below the lock and burst into flames. On impact the crew were flung from the huge six-engined stratojet, and managed to crawl over the footbridge to safety. The lock-keeper, being first on the scene, was able to patch up the crew until more help arrived. With smoke pouring from the stricken aircraft, and the orange glow of the blaze casting an eerie light, the fire crew from Faringdon must have had their most memorable call-out ever. Armed American military police sealed off the entire crash site for days while every last piece of wreckage was cleared. Was the aircraft's payload nuclear? It was certainly at the height of the Cold War, when missions were flown close to Soviet territory. The crew recovered from their injuries, apart from one who died at the crash site after being flung against a tree. A disgruntled local complained to the lock-keeper that armed guards prevented him from crossing the footbridge, and would he make the Thames Conservancy board do something about it. The lock-keeper was tempted to tell him it was doubtful that the Thames Conservancy could influence the Pentagon, but thought better of it!

Rushey weir and lock cottage, date unknown. The remote locks had the advantage of rare visits by the navigation inspectors and some lock-keepers took advantage of this fact to supplement their meagre income. One enterprising lock-keeper set up a sideline in wood-turning here and produced bedheads and legs. At another lock, the lock-keeper used to double up as the local postman. Whether any of this was known by the inspectors is unclear; possibly a blind eye was turned, provided there was no conflict of interest.

Shifford lock in the winter of 1958. Many isolated lock-houses such as Shifford suffered from a distinct lack of any decent form of heating; often they would only have a 'Rayburn' stove in the kitchen. These multi-fuel stoves supplied hot water and cooking facilities. Most of the fuel came down the river and only had to be dried out and stored in readiness for winter. Despite the heat provided by these stoves, the remainder of the house would often be draughty and very cold with ice forming on the inside of the windows!

Shifford lock, 1926. Most locks on the Thames were built at sites that had previously had a weir in one form or another, and although it appears that there were several weirs in the area, Shifford lock had the distinction of being built on a virgin site in about 1898.

The Board of Conservators on their annual inspection of Northmoor lock, 1920. Members of the public often made comment on how well the locks were presented, in particular the floral displays. There were inspections from the end of May (the Board Inspection) through to the last weekend in July (the Garden Inspection). Apart from personal pride, cups and monetary prizes were at stake, and the competition among lock-keepers was fierce. Some locks had an excellent location and layout enabling the lock-keeper to put on a fine display, while other locks had the exact opposite and a garden soil consisting of river dredgings, making winning any prize very difficult.

Strictly speaking, a breach of the bylaws prohibiting swimming in the lock. However, in the summer holidays of 1960 many of the local children came to Northmoor lock for a swim. With concrete steps and a known depth, it was probably far safer than swimming elsewhere in the river.

The ferry at Bablock Hythe in operation, 1960s. Here a Ford Prefect is crossing on the chain-operated ferry.

An Austin Healey Sprite and an MG Midget on the frozen Thames at Bablock Hythe ferry in the winter of 1962/3. What started out as a bit of fun on the ice ended up with both drivers racing one another. Inevitably, in the icy conditions both cars spun and crashed into each other causing minor damage.

Pinkhill lock, February 1932. When repairs or closure of a lock is forthcoming, a notice of the proposed works is posted at the locks in the district. Often, these are rarely read by the boating public. One gentleman who had not seen the closure notice for these repairs, approached the lock blasting his horn. The lock-keeper walked up the towpath and informed him that the lock was closed. 'What time do you open then, nine o'clock?' The lock-keeper replied, 'Yes sir, on the 1st of April!' Quite a shock to find an empty lock chamber before him, with the coping stones removed and the walls partly demolished. Note at the bottom of the lock the triangular timber framework. This was the original gate sill which gave the lock-gates support at the base and prevented distortion.

The flooded Thames at Swinford toll bridge, near Eynsham. This bridge was built at the site of a former ancient ferry to provide a short cut from Oxford to Witney. Unusually, the revenue taken in tolls from the bridge is exempt from income tax.

View of the old flash weir at Eynsham, looking downstream.

Work on the approach to Eynsham lock looking downstream in the winter of 1927/8. The works formed part of the Thames Conservancy's scheme to improve navigation and flood relief in the reach above Oxford. The lock-house was built of local stone at the same time.

The official opening day at Eynsham lock on 19 May 1928, a rather grand affair with marquees, press and local dignitaries. The opening ceremony was performed by the chairman of the Conservators, Lord Desborough. In the lock is the Board's steam launch *Donola*.

Eynsham flash weir, 1920s. Built in about 1886, this replaced an older weir some 100 m downstream from this point. The lower weir was in existence by about 1539, and was probably built by the local monks for catching fish. At that time it was referred to as 'Boldes' or 'Swithens'. Note the boat rollers to the left, a much quicker way of passing the weir for smaller boats.

Navigation Inspector Don Mackaskill taking a sounding of a shoal directly below Eynsham lock in 1959. While on patrol the launch scraped bottom, and a large shoal was discovered. The inspector then had to discover the extent of the shoal by donning waders, going over the side and taking soundings with a boathook. Severe flooding can sometimes sweep large amounts of material into the channel forming shoals. In this case the flow from the weir deposited a shoal directly below the lock. A potential hazard to navigation, it would have been quickly reported and later dredged clear.

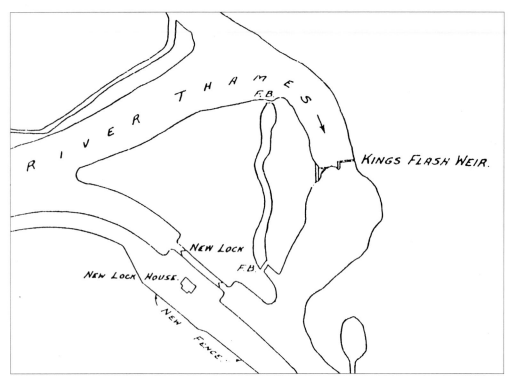

A Thames Conservancy map of Kings lock and the old flash pass. It is interesting to note the action of the river below the flash pass, scouring out the large pool downstream.

Differing slightly from a flash weir, Kings was a flash lock, sometimes referred to as a flash pass. It had a single pair of gates and three sets of paddles on each gate. Also visible is a small 'set' of paddles and rymers close to the wall on the right. The weir gates were raised by turning the handle on a toothed rack and wheel system.

Kings lock site, 1927. As improvements to navigation above Oxford were continued, the replacement for the flash lock at Kings was started. Seen here as rails in the field, within a short space of time the pound lock took shape.

Kings new lock with workmen reluctantly posing for the camera midway through the building process.

Later in 1927, and much progress has been made by the workmen on Kings lock. With the lock chamber nearly completed, the site is only recognizable by the trees in the background!

A distant view looking upstream to the new Kings lock and house on the left, and the old flash pass on the right.

Approaching Godstow lock in 1959, looking downstream. The cranes on either side of the river are in place to make a start on the A34 Oxford bypass bridge.

Essential works in progress at Godstow lock, 1924. Seen in the background are the ruins of the 'house of nunnes'. There was a legend attached to the nunnery that grew with each telling, of the murder of the mistress of King Henry II. This crime was supposedly carried out by Queen Eleanor of Aquitaine. King Henry installed his mistress Rosamund in a secretly located house protected by a knot-shaped maze. The jealous Queen penetrated these defences and poisoned Rosamund. Although interesting, it is unlikely to be true. Rosamund gave King Henry two sons and died of natural causes in about 1175.

Godstow lock in the early 1960s, with the lock-keeper engaged in the onerous task of scrubbing the lock walls. This had to be carried out on a regular basis to prevent the excessive growth of algae on the walls, something most boat owners are all too familiar with. Below the lock is the oldest part of Oxford, the natural flood plain of Port Meadow, which, despite four efforts in the last three hundred years to build houses, has remained virtually unchanged.

Osney lock, looking downstream, 1926.

Osney weir stream in the winter floods of 1928/9. The rear of the old-style lock cottage may be seen to the left, and the distant Oxford Gasworks. The lattice ironwork of the towpath bridge, still in use today, is just visible. The flooded meadows to the right were later to become the Osney Mead trading estate.

A camping punt in Osney lock with lock-keeper Albert Lloyd and friends, 1920s. In the background may be seen the older type of lock sign, reminiscent of a railway station, and the small whitewashed lock cottage.

A rare occasion, a number of lock-keepers together in one place. This photograph was taken at Number 1 district's annual dinner, 1960. This dinner was held at West Oxford Democrats club, Osney. Back row, left to right: Don Mackaskill (inspector), Ron Banks (Benson cruiser station), Jack Moffat (engineering foreman), -?-, Peter Scott (Rushey lock), Eric Eade (Clifton lock), Les Randall (Radcot lock), Alan Porter (Grafton lock), -?-, Alan Smith (Culham lock), Albert Wright (Pinkhill lock). Middle row: Lyn David (St John's lock), Chris Groves (assistant inspector), 'Nobby' Clarke (relief lock-keeper), Jack Sutherby (Days lock), Peter Smith (son of Percy Smith). Front row: George Newin (Abingdon lock), Arthur Rouse (Iffley lock), Ron Older (Sandford lock), Percy Smith (Northmoor lock).

The lock-keepers' children pose with their Christmas presents at the 1968 party. Arranged every year by lock-keeper Percy Smith, these were hugely popular and highly successful. The highlights (after presents) included jelly and ice-cream tea, meeting Santa and the release of a huge net of balloons from the ceiling. The resulting noise of these being burst by excited children was deafening!

The Thames Conservancy Board passing through Osney lock, 1920. The autocratic Board appointed lock-keepers to locks that suited the Board and the lock-keeper had little or no say in the matter. The author's grandfather was informed by letter in 1938 thus: 'The Conservators have decided to transfer you, during pleasure, to the post of Lock keeper at Romney lock, at the wages of £2. 2. 6 per week. . . .' The thought of a transfer, 'during pleasure', sounds most inconvenient!

'Time goes by, they say it alters, not at all if you work for Salters. Ring out the bell from every steeple, it makes no difference to boating people.' So the saying goes, and little seems to have changed at Salters Steamers premises near Folly bridge, Oxford. However, the rather elaborate building which was once the Boat House Tavern has been converted into flats. To the left of the other building in the photograph was a lock, traces of which may still be seen, along with a small arch under the road bridge for the towing path. It had one pair of gates below the present bridge, and a fall of up to a metre. The weir was situated upstream of Folly bridge at the head of the island, remnants of which were removed a few years ago, widening the navigation channel.

College barges on the Thames at Oxford, c. 1960. Based on the original design of the six London Guild barges of the nineteenth century, twenty-two were built for Oxford colleges. Although a Preservation Trust was formed in 1966, few examples have survived and the barges have been replaced by permanent buildings along the riverbank.

OXFORD TO HENLEY

With a great deal of history and some wonderful scenery, the Thames has much to offer the casual observer or the historian, with interest at every bend if one knows where to look. Navigation between Burcot and Oxford was once so difficult that barge cargoes often had to be unloaded and sent by road. So rife were complaints that one of the first of many governing bodies was set up, the Oxford–Burcot Commission. The Commission had little real power but still built the first of the 'modern' pound locks in about 1630 at Iffley, Sandford and the sadly neglected lock on Swift Ditch above Abingdon lock.

These early successes later led to the more powerful but unwieldy Thames Navigation Commission (Act of 1751). This body did much to improve the standard of navigation and had greater powers to purchase land, flash weirs and also to build pound locks. With the formation of the Thames Conservancy in 1857, came two notable firsts. Mapledurham lock was the first lock to be converted from hand power to an experimental electro-mechanical system in 1956. Five years later, Shiplake lock received the now familiar and more reliable hydraulic system.

Iffley mill and weir looking upstream from the towpath. Dating back to 1170, the mill was bought by Lincoln College in 1445 and let with the proviso of a day's fishing annually for the rector and fellows of the college. This photograph was certainly taken before 20 May 1908, when fire destroyed most of the mill. Iffley was one of three locks built in about 1632 and some of the original stonework of the lock is still noticeable above the current weir. The wooden bridge to the left crossed the old weir pool, which was drained and partly filled to accommodate the new lock and boat rollers, completed in 1924.

The drained weir pool and old lock-house at Iffley, c. 1923. Difficult to visualize today, this scene looks downstream with the main river out of sight on the left. On the left and in the foreground are the remains of the original overfall into the pool. The new lock is taking shape in the centre of the view.

More or less the same view some months later. Work has progressed considerably with access to the boat rollers nearing completion on the right. Iffley lock as it is today may be seen in the background with the new entrance channel to the lock. The old lock-house is shored up with timber prior to demolition.

One of the first users of the new lock at Iffley, an eight from Oxford University. It was probably photographed in early 1924, as the lock was officially opened on 19 July 1924 by the Right Honourable Lord Desborough, KCVO, Chairman of the Conservators.

Sandford mill and lock looking upstream, 1969. This lock, like Iffley above it, was one of the first pound locks built by the Oxford–Burcot Commission in about 1632. Sandford mill on the right once ground corn and later became a paper mill. The mills were demolished for redevelopment, but the mill leat still discharges water under the properties. Entering the deepest lock on the Thames can still be a daunting experience, but before changes to an underfloor filling system in the early 1970s it was positively terrifying, with water shooting out in huge arcs from the top sluices.

Empty of its water for essential repairs in 1969, Sandford lock does not seem quite so powerful. This lock was built in 1836 next to the original which was later sold to the mill-owners for £50. Note the timbers and the rubbing posts at the sides of the lock below the water line.

Looking down on to the sluice operating gear on the lock gates at Sandford lock. A design of simplicity and effectiveness, the sluices were originally raised by turning the handles of a capstan similar to a ship's wheel. Later, this method was replaced with hydraulic rams operated from a control pedestal, although some locks upriver are still manually operated.

The wooden towpath bridge and flooded meadows below Abingdon lock in the winter of 1959, with the distant spire of St Helen's church just noticeable. Imagine popping out for your milk and papers in these conditions!

Abingdon lock, winter 1962/3. It is essential that the weirs are kept clear of obstructions and are free to operate, and in January 1963 the weir was iced up solid. In sub-zero temperatures the lock-keeper had to descend on to the weir apron and chip away at the accumulated ice. In conditions that health and safety regulations would not allow today, alone and without flotation aid or safety lines, he slipped and fell into the icy waters above the weir. The extreme plunge in temperature was described as literally taking his breath away but despite this he somehow scrambled up on to the weir platform to safety. Completely soaked, very cold and with waders full of freezing water, he had to run to the lock-house as quickly as possible. Tearing off the waders on the way, the lock-keeper ran in stockinged feet across the ice and snow to the lock-house. Here, he thought, hot water would be available and all would be well. He was wrong however; even the water pipes had frozen solid and the best that could be managed was some hot water boiled up in a kettle. Fortunately he eventually thawed out with no ill effects, sometime in April!

'It has been noticed that certain lock and weir keepers appear to spend much time in dispensing ginger beer and other refreshments to members of the public and I have been directed to place a curb on the practice.' So said Chief Inspector Laurie in his handwritten orders of 1906, yet for many lock-keepers this was a way of earning extra money. Many locks had tea gardens such as this one at Abingdon, or sold garden produce to the boaters, while others even set up small shops. This practice has fallen in and out of favour over the years with each successive change of management.

Two members of the Upper Thames Patrol with their young recruit on board *Induna* below Abingdon bridge, September 1940. Formed as a waterborne version of 'Dad's Army' to patrol the river, the Upper Thames Patrol consisted mainly of lock-keepers. The early uniform seen in this photograph was made up from whatever clothes came to hand. Later they were issued the same uniform as the regular Home Guard, but retained a distinctive metal badge bearing the arms of the Thames Conservancy with UTP underneath and UTP shoulder flashes. When the uniform first appeared, some jokers suggested that the initials UTP stood for 'Up The Pub' which may have had a degree of truth in it!

The *Grand Duchess*, half submerged in Abingdon weir stream, *c.* 1964. Bought by a local farmer for storing hay, the largest of the ex-Salters fleet was moored on land upstream and opposite the lock. Here it remained for many months, slowly taking in water and being pumped out on a daily basis by the farmer, until one day when the poor old steamer finally started to sink rapidly. Noticing this, the lock-keeper telephoned the farmer, who in turn called out the fire brigade for help as his pump was unable to cope with the volume of water pouring in through the portholes. Somehow the message went out that a steamer full of passengers was sinking at the lock. Pandemonium ensued with fire engines, ambulances and police cars racing to the lockside, while on the other side of the river the *Duchess* was still shipping water at an alarming rate. The firemen steadfastly refused to leave until they had installed a pump on the steamer, and the unfortunate lock-keeper was press-ganged into urgent ferry duties with minutes to go before the steamer went down. Not designed to carry large pumps as well as several burly firemen, the lock punt was rowed precariously across the river with very little freeboard. In the nick of time the pumps were manhandled aboard the stricken steamer and started. At first they had little effect, then slowly but surely they began to make headway and many hours later the *Duchess* eventually refloated. She was later moved to the Abbey mill stream and into a custom-made refuge excavated in the bank, but she sank here too. In later years she was towed to Sandford, where she sank once more and broke up; a sad end for the once grand old lady.

The effect of the elements and water on the old timbers of Culham weir may be seen here, photographed in 1961. Many of the original Thames weirs were constructed of timber and lasted very well, but eventually the wood deteriorated and the weirs had to be replaced.

Possibly heading for a concert at Nuneham House, near Oxford, a floating orchestra platform fills all of Culham lock. The pontoons on either side were lowered to provide a considerable area on which to play.

Culham lock, 1958, and the unusual sight of two lock-houses next to each other. Once the new house on the left was finished, the lock-keeper was able to move in and the old house was later demolished.

With the entire contents of a lock-house under a tarpaulin in a barge, moving house in 1961 was a matter of loading the barge at one lock and unloading at the new destination. In this case, the barge is approaching Culham lock en route from Clifton Hampden to Abingdon. With vehicular access to some locks difficult or non-existent, this method was often used as a 'door-to-door' service.

Clifton weir iced up in the winter of 1961, with ice floes on the river. Imagine having to walk to the weir in the dead of night to work alone in such conditions.

Another view of the frozen weir at Clifton. Despite the ice on the weir and the distinct lack of any form of health and safety requirements, accidents were rare among lock-keepers.

Clifton lock, *c.* 1898: probably a family portrait, of the lock-keeper James Bossom on the lock-gate, and his son Charles on the edge of the lock, together with his wife, mother, daughter and family dog. Charles was to follow in his father's footsteps and become Clifton lock-keeper in the 1930s. The old lock-house seen here was replaced by the present one in 1929. Close examination of the photograph reveals a tame jackdaw upon James' left shoulder.

Charles Bossom, Clifton lock-keeper, on the 'lasher' weir behind the lock house in the early 1930s. When Charles died in post at the age of 47, his coffin was placed on a barge, then poled downstream to Clifton church by his fellow lock-keepers and inspectors.

The author, aged 5, on board the 'Cliftonville Express' at Clifton lock. Made by his father out of bits and pieces of driftwood and the ever-present oil drum, the engine was a great success. The realistic-looking steam coming out of the funnel was produced by lighting an oily rag and allowing it to smoulder.

Unlike a book-keeping error which can remain hidden for years, an error in river management will always become apparent. However, once a weir is said to be fully drawn, that is, all available tackle is out, then little else can be done but to wait for the water to subside. Lock-keeper Eric Eade 'at sea' in the meadows near Clifton, waiting.

Looking downstream from the lock to Clifton bridge across flooded meadows, 1960. In daylight it is difficult to tell where the towpath ends and the river begins. Now try to imagine wading from the bridge to the lock in pitch darkness, knowing that the lock-keeper is bleeding badly and needs help. This scenario occurred in 1958 when assistant inspector Chris Groves made the most hazardous walk of his life to help the Clifton lock-keeper who was in desperate trouble. By the light of his torch Chris waded up the uneven towpath against the fast-flowing water. He had to feel his way slowly with a stick for the edge of the main river to avoid being swept away, knowing that any mistake could spell disaster for both men. Still bleeding profusely from a broken vein in his nose, the lock-keeper watched helplessly as the flickering light of his rescuer moved slowly nearer. After what must have seemed an eternity, Chris arrived safely at the lock-house to everyone's relief, after a very harrowing walk. That drama over, he then faced the task of evacuating the lock-keeper and his family. Time was of the essence as the lock-keeper had lost a great deal of blood and was feeling weak and light-headed. Chris had to row an unfamiliar boat, in the dark, across a very fast weir stream to the Long Wittenham road and the safety of a waiting car. All was well in the end, as a result of Chris' heroic efforts.

Concrete blocks guarding the Thames next to the Long Wittenham road. These and the numerous pill boxes positioned along the Thames formed a line of defence across southern England in the event of a German invasion. Note also the wooden letterbox for Clifton lock which saved the postman the long walk to the lock.

Construction of the new weir at Days. The 1947 flood mark is just visible.

The new Days weir after completion. As soon as this work was finished, the ever-present fishermen moved in for the excellent pike and barbel fishing to be found in weir streams.

Looking upstream towards Days lock, with the recently reconstructed weir on the left. Unusually, the lock-house was not built adjacent to the lock. For many, Days lock and 'Pooh Sticks' are synonymous. During his residency here as lock-keeper, Lyn David raised a six-figure sum for the RNLI by selling books and staging the now famous International 'Pooh Sticks' contest on the bridge below the lock. For his fund-raising efforts he was awarded the OBE.

Keen Edge ferry house near Shillingford, shortly before demolition in 1961. When towpaths changed banks, the Thames Conservancy was obliged to provide a ferry service for people and animals. On one occasion a bull had charged passionately across the river to service a herd of heifers on the other side. Exhausted, the bull was unable to make the return journey by the same method and the ferryman's barge was needed. The farmer said to the ferryman, 'we'll go behind him and we'll drive him on to the barge, then we'll . . . ' At this point the ferryman interrupted, 'No, *you* will catch your bull, *you* will rope him and *you* will lead him on to the ferry barge. Then I will row you both over, and *you* will take your bull a very long way away from me!'

Shillingford wharf, September 1958. Nearby may be found quite a record of Thames floods. At most locks two flood marks may usually be found, 1894 and 1947. Here on a wall, just up from the river, is an iron flood marker with eight floods marked: 1809 (the highest), 1894, 1821, 1768, 1947, 1852, 1929 and 1875. There are also two stones set into the wall here, both of which are inscribed 'up to this stone the water run'. One appears to be an original.

Shillingford Bridge and toll-house, 1937. Records indicate a bridge here as early as 1301; however, the bridge in this photograph replaced a ferry and at least two other bridges. Tolls were levied to cross here until 1874, when the responsibility to maintain the bridge passed to local authorities. Shortly after this photograph was taken, the toll-house was demolished.

With money in short supply in the 1930s, amusement for the Benson lock-keeper's son was the simple pleasure of paddling about in an old tin bath.

'Stick your chest out for the photographer, son, or I'll beat you with this chain' could be the caption to this photograph of the author's grandfather and father beside Benson lock punt in the 1930s.

The flooded weir platform at Benson, 1959, with the lock-keeper John Jeffrey making his way out to the village. Note the beginning of improvements to health and safety with a safety line strung across the weir, although there is no sign of a life jacket.

Benson weir in the summer of 1928. Compare this with the water levels in the winter.

Memorandum

TELEGRAPHIC ADDRESS:
ONSERVANCY, ESTRAND, LONDON,"
TELEPHONES:
TEMPLE BAR 5855 (3 LINES.)

From the Secretary,

Thames Conservancy.

2 & 3, Norfolk Street,

68/36   *Strand, W. C. 2.*

To   23rd January, 1936.

                    Mr. J.W. Eade,
                        Lock-keeper,
                        BENSON LOCK.

Dear Eade,

It has been reported to me, and I have also seen in the Press an account of the prompt and praiseworthy action taken by you on Sunday, the 12th ultimo, to rescue from a position of much danger near the weir, two men.

I can appreciate the risk you ran in your endeavour to reach and save the men, who were clinging to the 'Danger' pile, and I am very pleased with the meritorious manner in which you so successfully acted on the occasion.

J. Geary

Inspector Geary commends the Benson lock-keeper for his heroic rescue of two men. The full story is recounted opposite.

The river in flood can be dangerous, as two fishermen discovered at Benson in 1936. Hearing shouts for help, the lock-keeper discovered two men clinging desperately to the 'Danger' board upstream of the weir. Local fishermen, William Aldridge and Joey Lane, had lost control of their boat and were swept broadside into the pile in front of the weir. The boat broke up just after they scrambled to the relative safety of the 'Danger' board. The quick-thinking lock-keeper gathered up metal, heavy weights and some rope to make a dragging anchor. He then shouted to the terrified men that he would get them but they would have to jump when he said and without hesitation. With daylight fading, he rowed upstream along the bank, then moved out into the main stream with the anchor dragging. Even with this dragging, the punt was moving at an alarming rate towards the weir. The crucial moment arrived. 'Jump!' he cried, and one man crashed into the punt. 'You!' he shouted, and the other man leapt. He landed awkwardly, almost going over the side, but the lock-keeper grabbed his collar and dragged him in. With both men safely in, the anchor was cut and the punt rowed perilously close to the face of the weir to the nearest bank. The Conservators expressed their thanks with a gratuity of two guineas. The grateful men gave the lock-keeper a bushel of Blenheim apples.

The launching of a boat down the slipway at the Springfield works of Saunders boatyard, 1902. Boats of every kind were built in the Goring area by the Saunders family from about 1830 onwards. Sam Saunders once boasted that his punt poles were unbreakable and he would pay £20 to anyone who broke one during normal use. As far as it is known, he never did have to pay out. The family business eventually moved to the Isle of Wight where they built flying boats and latterly hovercraft as Saunders-Roe.

The Leathern Bottle, c. 1890. In the seventeenth and eighteenth centuries pilgrims made their way to this riverside pub to partake of the waters, said to cure rashes of the eyes and skin and 'ache of corns'. Modern-day pilgrims still make their way here, perhaps for different reasons.

Roses climbing up the old lock cottage at Cleeve, *c*. 1900. This was the public face of lock-keeping, quaint and charming. The reality, however, was different, with poor wages and hard physical work in all weathers.

Cleeve lock in the winter of 1962, not a good time to be a lock-keeper. Scenes like this visibly demonstrate that even in relatively recent times harsh weather made life difficult for the lock-keeper and his family.

The back of Cleeve lock cottage and weir in 1958, with anglers enjoying the fishing in the weir pool. One of the oldest surviving original lock cottages, it was eventually demolished and the new house was occupied by 1960.

Goring lock undergoing rebuild, winter 1922. The flooding made the work even more difficult for the gang of workmen.

Goring lock and house surrounded by water in the floods of 1947. Note the unusual arrangement of three sets of lock-gates.

The toll-house on the bridge between Goring and Streatley, before 1923 when the bridge was finally freed from tolls. Seen here at the toll-gate are the toll collectors, Mr and Mrs Holder.

The weir at Whitchurch, probably *c.* 1900, with the mill and lock visible in the background.

With the Thames flooding more frequently than today, scenes like this one, at the Swan pub and Whitchurch weir in early January 1925, were not unusual. Going out for a drink could be quite hazardous.

District relief Peter Gough returning from working on Mapledurham weir, carrying a weed drag. In the foreground the paddle and rymer arrangement of the weir can be seen, with spare paddles leaning against the railing. Tragically, Peter was to lose his life in a freak accident clearing his weir at Shiplake in January 1982.

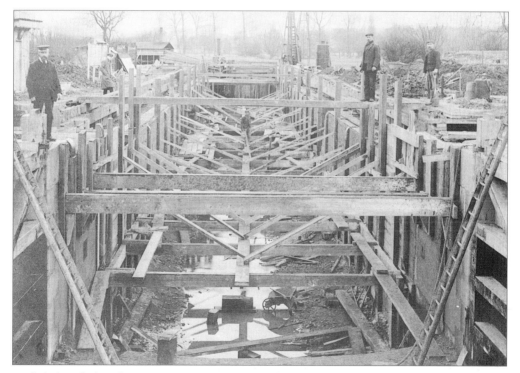

Mapledurham lock undergoing repairs in 1908, showing the elaborate method of supporting the sides of the lock. In order to prevent the collapse of the lock walls when the pressure was released, it was necessary to support the walls with huge timbers.

The iron lattice-work of Caversham bridge as it looked in 1869. Behind it are the remains of the older bridge built in two halves of brick and timber, the result of a dispute between the corporation of Reading and the county of Oxfordshire. On board the ferry are a pony and trap and a milk cart from Mapledurham dairy. From the waterman's white cottage on the Caversham side, boats were 'let on hire at moderate charges'.

'Bucket and spoon' dredging in operation upstream of Reading bridge. Probably laid on for the benefit of the photographer, this method of dredging the river was slow and laborious. One operator pushed the 'bucket' into the mud on the river bed, while the other winched the attached chain along, drawing the mud into the bucket. This was then swung aboard as seen here, to be emptied into the flat. The whole process was then repeated over and over again.

A closer view of the bucket and spoon, also showing the chain and winch used to drag the device along the river bed. Note that two of the four ryepeck poles are angled into the river bed to stabilize the flat while dredging was carried out.

Caversham lock flooded, with water pouring over the gates. This flood is probably in 1903.

Reading bridge, September 1923. Even though it was designed to withstand the required load of 293 tons, concern was expressed as to the strength of the structure. To prove it was strong enough, a number of steam rollers, traction engines and loaded lorries were driven on to the bridge to test it. If the bridge had failed the test at this point, the consequences would have been very serious indeed.

Repairs to Sonning lock, 1903. On the lock side to the right is the inspector, Mr Laurie, and the lock-keeper to the left leaning on the pile is Mr Waller.

Sonning house weir, November 1957. At the time it was the deepest paddle and rymer weir on the Thames. To give the rymers extra weight they were clad with iron and it took four men to pitch them! It does appear that a great deal of potential energy is available from the Thames weirs when they are fully open. A scheme was once looked at to harness this energy and a feasibility study commissioned. However, there has been little progress on this matter and the potential is literally running away.

Shiplake lock, 1907.

Donola in Shiplake lock during the Board of Conservators' annual lock inspection. *Donola* was originally named *Lodona* but had the name changed to avoid confusion with another Thames Conservancy launch, the *Loddon*. *Donola* made her last voyage down the Thames after forty-nine years service on 29 April 1969. Her destination was the Neptune Hall of the Greenwich Maritime Museum.

Two of the Thames Conservancy divers with their friend 'Guy' outside Shiplake lock-house, 5 November 1961. Given the amount of rubbish that found its way down the river, most locks had huge bonfires on 5 November. The heat from one such bonfire was so intense that it melted an aluminium saucepan.

The two sons of the Shiplake lock-keeper, Roger and Stephen Gough, panning for treasure at the bottom of the lock. During the £11,000 renovation in 1960/61 they found a King George III penny, £3-worth of other coins, four pairs of glasses and even a set of false teeth!

Thames Conservancy diver Johnny Cook, wearing the traditional diving suit with lead weights and heavy boots. As part of the gang involved in lock and weir maintenance the diver's role was varied, from examining piling condition to the removal of underwater obstructions in locks.

Looking down on Shiplake lock before work commenced on the conversion to hydraulic power in 1961. The lock-keeper, Peter Gough, had a habit of climbing up any crane that was available to take photographs, and this is one of his.

Lashbrook ferry, 1926. One of many ferries on the Thames that came into being as a result of property owners refusing to give permission for the towing path to cross their land. It therefore fell to the Conservancy to provide a means of crossing the river. With the need for ferries dying out, all the Thames Conservancy ferries were eventually closed. However, traces of their existence may still be found on old maps and in road names such as Ferry Lane.

Lashbrook ferry house flooded, 1925. The perils of living so close to the Thames can be seen here as the ferryman evacuates his furniture via a window.

A fine summer's day will always bring out the boats. Here a varied collection of boats patiently wait to pass through Marsh lock in the early 1960s. Not all boaters are patient, and this no doubt prompted the lock-keeper's lament from the *Lock to Lock Times* of 1888:

> We're them as works on the river all day,
> For them as comes on the river to play,
> It's precious little of fun is ours,
> For it ain't confined to regular hours,
> But any moment, from morn to night,
> We have to put it with all our might,
> As soon as ever a boat gets nigh,
> We're sure to hear the same old cry:–
> 'Lock, lock, lock!'
> It always is the same,
> 'Lock, lock, lock!'
> Till we're sick of the blooming name!
>
> The river usen't to be like this,
> And then our life was downright bliss;
> Then there was only a barge or two,
> And mostly little enough to do.
> But now it's getting too mighty strong,
> The gates is going the whole day long;
> Our hands gets hot, and our throats is dry
> With looking arter that mortal cry:
> 'Lock, lock, lock!'
> It always is the same;
> 'Lock, lock, lock!'
> No praise, but oftener blame.

HENLEY TO OLD WINDSOR

Amateur regattas, the picturesque sweep of Marlow weir, Quarry Woods, Winter Hill, the splendid reach at Cliveden, the woods at Cookham lock, the very popular Boulters, Windsor Castle and Eton College, views from the river that have remained largely unchanged over the centuries. Not all has remained unchanged, however. Housing pressures have resulted in the loss of some working mills. Temple, Marlow, Cookham, Ray Mill near Boulters and Tangier Mill just below Romney lock have all been developed for residential housing. At Cookham, Hedsor water was once the main channel of the Thames and involved the Commissioners in protracted and expensive litigation with the owner of Hedsor wharf, Lord Boston. When Cookham lock and cut were built in about 1830 and his Lordship lost revenue from towpath tolls, he sued and won on appeal. Matters deteriorated a few years later when a weir was built, preventing access to Hedsor wharf. More litigation ensued, resulting in some compensation and inclusion of a flash pass in the weir. The upper weir was rebuilt and eel bucks were built at the tail of the reach, thus closing Hedsor Water to navigation and privatizing the water.

The Thames Conservancy patrol launches, *Colne*, *Seven Springs*, *Ember* and *Windrush*, moored up at Henley in the early 1960s. The role of the inspectors at the Regatta was mainly to keep the course clear and escort through-traffic past in convoys. They also had to ensure that everyone was fed and ventured into town to buy the food. Catering was provided by the crew of the *Windrush* and everyone slept in a marquee pitched at Fawley.

Lock-keeper Peter Gough and two helpers on patrol at Henley in a Thames Conservancy dinghy. In order to maintain a clear passage through for boats not attending the Regatta, volunteer lock-keepers manned guard boats such as this at the top and bottom of the course to control the extra river traffic.

The famous Amateur Rowing Regatta finish-line at Henley in the early 1960s. Note the funfair and helter-skelter on the opposite bank, behind the marquees.

Work in progress, straightening Henley regatta course at Temple island, 1924. To the left is the old river bank and piles, while new piles are driven with the so-called 'ringing engine'. This work widened the course by some 23 m.

Hambledon lock, 1926. Situated at the end of the Henley regatta course, it is said that the very first University Boat Race between Cambridge and Oxford started from here, not once, but twice, owing to a collision.

The Thames Conservancy launch, *Windrush*, in Hambledon lock on the way to Henley regatta. Aboard is HRH Queen Elizabeth who would later present the prizes in the stewards' enclosure, the Queen Mother, Princess Margaret, Lord Snowdon and Lord and Lady Nugent. The avid royalist filming the event by the lock gate could have been in for a shock when the gate was closed!

The brick-built Hambledon lock, empty in 1970 for improvement work. This lock has been the subject of recent work to provide an under-floor filling system, a method which produces less turbulence in the lock, enabling boats to be lifted quickly and safely.

Aston ferry and ferryman Mr Hawkes, 1926. Situated below Hambledon lock, this ferry was once what was termed a rope ferry, whereby the ferry boat or flat was pulled from one side to the other by a rope stretched across the river. The rope proved to be a hazard to navigation and was later replaced by a chain or cable laid on the riverbed. Most ferries were discontinued after the Second World War.

Hurley old lock-house in 1958, shortly before demolition. The lock beams seen here had a life of many years and were regularly maintained and painted. They provided a convenient seat for the lock-keeper and the public; sometimes up to eight people sat on them, waiting for boats. Eventually, however, the rot sets in, usually at the joint with the gate. On one occasion, one of the beams was due for replacement and the lock-keeper had reported this to the engineering yard where a new one was waiting to be fitted. Late one summer evening, a young couple sat on the beam while the lock-keeper was indoors. All was fine until the couple started to bounce up and down on the beam. As they stopped bouncing, the old beam finally gave up and cracked at the joint. Slowly the couple were lowered to the ground as the wood split still further. Meanwhile, indoors, the lock-keeper had witnessed all of this with ever increasing laughter. After much discussion and red faces, the man knocked on the door of the lock-house and said, 'Excuse me, but I'm afraid I've just broken your lock.' The lock-keeper told him that it didn't really matter and not to be concerned. The man was insistent that the lock-keeper have a look at the damage and together they crossed to the broken beam, now resting on the ground. The girl's face was crimson with embarrassment and her eyes were fixed firmly on the ground. The lock-keeper surveyed the broken beam thoughtfully for some moments and then asked for help. Anxious to please, the man jumped at the chance to make amends. Fetching a crosscut saw from the office, the unlikely pair then cut off the beam completely. The lock-keeper thanked him for helping and said goodbye. 'But don't you want my name and address?' queried the man. The lock-keeper told them both to disappear and to forget all about the incident. It is unlikely that would have been the case.

Temple lock cottage, 1958, shortly before replacement. Although showing signs of its age, it still had a certain charm about it. On the left-hand wall near the roof appears to be a water tank, probably either filled by rainwater from the roof or with river water. Many lock cottages had no mains water supply and the lock-keeper and his family had to drink river water. The water was pumped by hand into a tank for the sediment to settle out, then through gravel, pea grit and charcoal. At this point, chlorine was added along with another tablet and it was then filtered through charcoal once more. After this the water was safe to drink. One lock-keeper recalls visitors from more civilized parts using the drinking-water tap to wash their hands, while he was outside pumping like crazy to keep up with the demand!

Ice-skating on the frozen Thames above Marlow bridge, c. 1895. This photograph makes a welcome change from the usual photographs of a coach-and-four on the ice.

Aerial photograph, looking downstream to Marlow mills, lock and weir, *c.* 1946. There was a mill established here by 1086, and three more by 1723. The whole site was up for sale in 1939 for £2,000.

Looking downstream to Marlow lock in 1927, when work was carried out to improve the lock. During the excavations here the original land ties which supported the lock walls were uncovered almost 7 m back from the lock sides.

Dutch sailing barge moored above Marlow lock, 1958.

The Thames Conservancy launch *Loddon* moored above Marlow lock. In the background is the elegant house, Thames Lawn. This house served as a backdrop for a dramatic scene in a television series in the late 1960s. After taking most of the day in setting up, a cabin cruiser was blown up in spectacular fashion for a dream sequence. Despite knowing there was to be an massive explosion, all of the spectators jumped out of their skins!

A racing eight in front of Marlow weir, *c.* 1968, a calm and peaceful scene with the church and bridge in the background. The danger of this weir in high water is apparent, as a crew from the local grammar school, Borlase, was to find out. The first the lock-keeper knew about an eight broadside and entangled on his weir was a phone call from the police, followed by their swift arrival. The eight was well and truly stuck and in imminent danger of breaking up from water pressure on the hull. Four men looked on helplessly at nine very frightened boys out of reach on the weir guard piles. The plan was to evacuate them via the lock ladder after it had been dropped across to the chains between the piles. Someone was despatched to fetch the aluminium ladder. Everybody was doubtful and to fail would have been disastrous. Would the plan work? What if the chains were missed? Supposing they broke? Would the boys' movement upset the boat? The whole situation was fraught with danger. With darkness closing in and time running out the difficult decision had to be made by the lock-keeper, and quickly. Plan B was decided upon, which was to close all of the weir tackle in one go and for the boys to row off in the short window of slack water before it built up again. The police were briefed on how to drop the weir tackle and the boys were told above the roar of the water what to expect. When the signal came, shock waves ran up the weir as fourteen hand radials were dropped and two large gates closed rapidly in succession. It was unlikely that this strategy had been tried before, and its effects were unknown – fully drawn to fully closed in a matter of minutes! Fortunately the plan worked and the crew was able to push off from the weir and row safely away. Their part in the drama played out, the police departed too. Then the lock-keeper and his assistant had to work into the night to open all of the weir tackle again to prevent a flood.

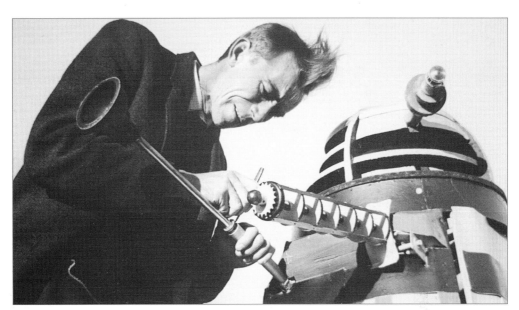

This 'dalek' was built in 1967 for the lock-keepers' children's Christmas party. Its appearance caused pandemonium and scuffles among the children in their desire to be inside it. Inside was a seat, handles to operate the arms, and a rotating top. The whole contraption was designed to be foot-propelled, but all the children rushed around and pushed it along excitedly. Built by Eric Eade, lock-keeper at Marlow, out of driftwood and metal from an oil drum rescued off the weir, it also incorporated a sink plunger, a bicycle sprocket and a car's indicator. Note the mesh at the front to see out of and the side door for access.

Marlow lock undergoing repairs, 1927. The old lock-house on the left was replaced in about 1959 with the present house. One lock-keeper in the 1960s discovered steps while digging in the garden. Excited by his find, he enlisted the help of the permanent assistant to dig deeper. On and on they dug, until at last they were surprised to find something . . . a rather awful smell! It seems that they had dug up buried treasure all right, the cesspit of the old lock-house!

Marlow lock from the air, June 1967. The white mill-houses seen here were built in a similar style to the former mills on this site, demolished two years earlier. Note the mill leat still discharging water under these houses.

The notorious flood of 1947, almost covering the Bourne End to Marlow railway line. In order to avoid a repeat in later years, the line was raised 150 mm.

The cattle ferry at Spade Oak, near Bourne End, late 1940s. The ferryman seen here, Mr John Chittenden, was the last Thames Conservancy employee to reside in the ferry house at Spade Oak. The chain-operated cattle ferry was only used when the main ferry punt was busy. Note the white painted lee board, used to stabilize the boat.

Cockmarsh bathing place, near Bourne End. One of many bathing places on the Thames that were popular until the war, it fell into decline through lack of use and the opening of municipal swimming baths.

The picturesque *My Lady* ferry, spring 1958. It was rented by the Thames Conservancy from Lord Astor for the peppercorn rent of 1s per annum. Many lock-keepers started their careers as ferrymen working for the Thames Conservancy. Although wages and conditions were poor, there was the incentive of a cottage attached to the job. Occasionally, and very unofficially, the game-keepers would give the ferryman's wife a rabbit or hare for the pot when they returned from Whites farm on the opposite bank.

My Lady ferry near Cookham, January 1958. The cottage was very small and had no bathroom, so in order to have a bath the ferryman and his family would have to carry a bucket of coal to Lodge Cottage, the home of a retired Cliveden gardener, and bathe there.

Hedsor weir in 1937, showing the dilapidated wooden structure in Hedsor water. Closer examination reveals that the wooden gates on the far side were winched up on spindles by either rope or chain. The near side appears to be a flash pass similar to the one at Kings, with the paddles and rymers out.

Hedsor mill, *c.* 1900.

Cookham lock undergoing essential maintenance work. The original lock was completed in 1830 and, as outlined earlier, caused huge problems for the Thames Commissioners. The lock had effectively bypassed the flash weir in Hedsor Water, resulting in loss of tolls for the owner, Lord Boston.

In order to carry out improvements to Boulters lock, the lock first had to have all of the water pumped out as seen here.

The engineers involved in the works at Boulters lock examine the operating mechanism for the lock-gates, *c.* 1912. In the background to the left, the lock-keeper takes a passing interest.

The boat escalator at Boulters lock, *c.* 1912. The lock was one of the busiest on the Thames and to cope with the extra traffic this escalator was built to bypass the lock instead of the more conventional boat rollers. In the background is the small building that housed the engine to drive the escalator.

Boulters lock looking downstream, *c.* 1937, an unusually quiet time at one of the river's busiest locks. Note the old-style capstan for operating the gates.

A crowd of boaters entering Boulters lock, *c.* 1912, under the wooden shuttering formers for the elegant bridge at the tail of the lock. The lock-keeper is looking under the bridge, no doubt concerned whether all the boats will fit into the lock.

A dramatic photograph of a boat on fire at Bushnell's boatyard, Maidenhead. A minor fault can trigger this type of fire in seconds, and with gas cylinders on board as well as fuel the risk of explosion is great. The consequences of this happening in a lock full of other boats does not bear thinking about. Fortunately, this sort of incident occurs infrequently, mainly owing to increased vigilance by hire companies, boatyards and the navigation inspectorate.

The flooded Ray Mill road in Maidenhead. Scenes such as these were commonplace until 1965, when a flood relief scheme was implemented.

Bray weir, 1925. Many strange things turn up on Thames weirs including the bodies of suicide victims. One lock-keeper regretted the day he pushed a sack over his weir, thinking that it contained a body. The sack eventually turned up at the next weir below where a more conscientious lock-keeper retrieved it. Instead of a body, the sack held several stolen furs, and the grateful owners substantially rewarded the lock-keeper for his honesty.

A view of the stream before it was widened in 1965 for the Maidenhead flood relief scheme, looking upstream from Bray road bridge.

The same view after work had been carried out. While there were benefits to residents from this work, the earlier stream was far more pleasing to the eye.

Boveney lock with the Eton 'wet bobs' waiting to go downstream. Ahead of most locks, although not visible in this photo, are large 'Danger' boards warning boaters to be wary of the weir stream. One particular day, a large hire boat approached the lock at speed and out of position to enter the lock. Seeing the lock too late, the skipper swung the wheel over and the strong stream caught him broadside, smashing the boat hard into the 'Danger' board. From inside the boat screams could be heard over the sound of breaking crockery. The skipper then immediately drove the boat forward and succeeded in smashing the cabin window. More screams from inside. Freeing the boat, he tried again. This time the boat hit the board sideways, taking chunks out of the boat's woodwork. All this noise had attracted the lock-keeper's attention, and he was shouting to the skipper, who couldn't hear above the racket. Next, the skipper decided to go astern, but being at the wrong angle for this, succeeded in putting the other end of the 'Danger' board through another window, showering glass inside. At this crash the screaming from inside the cabin became hysterical. The skipper went astern again, this time so successfully that he shot backwards into a reed bed. As the stern jammed in, the bows swung downstream pointing straight at the weir. Dad needed help, so his son pulled on a branch in an attempt to bring the boat closer to the bank. Blissfully unaware of his son's efforts, Dad attempted a dangerous U-turn across the face of the weir. By now the helpless lock-keeper was jumping up and down and yelling NO! at the top of his voice. The boat shot forward and the boy hung grimly from the branch. The branch snapped, dropping him in the river. Without knowing, Dad then nearly reversed over him. Luckily, the boy managed to scramble ashore with the stern line and tie up. Finally, the lock-keeper's instructions to tie up the bows as well were heard. With the bows still facing towards the weir, the next move was to let the stern line go, swinging the bows around to face upstream. That done, the crew were told to go below, make a pot of tea and calm down. The next instruction from the lock-keeper was for the crew to head upstream away from the weir and approach the lock close to the bank. Success at last! They entered the lock with no dramas at all, apart from all the broken glass and crockery and some very wounded pride. Unfortunately, the lock keeper then had to report them for damaging Thames Conservancy property, namely the 'Danger' board that had taken such a battering!

Romney weir, 30 December 1927. Heavily laden with timber and probably caught by the strong stream, the barge *Faith* was swept broadside across the weir. With the river already running high, a barge allowed to block the weir for too long could rapidly cause severe flooding.

Romney lock, 1946. In the lock a 100-ton barge has collided with the lock-gate on the left, causing severe damage. The handrail from the gate is lying on the towpath and the gate has been winched back, the cables just visible. This incident caused severe delays to other users while repairs were carried out.

'Jim' Eade at Romney lock in the 1940s, the effects of a life at sea and on the river apparent in his weather-beaten face. It is not known if wearing trousers in this manner was regulation or not! Like many lock-keepers of the time he was a retired navy man, in this case Chief Petty Officer and holder of the Distinguished Service Medal. At one time he was seamanship instructor at the Royal Navy College at Osborne, Isle of Wight. Among his pupils was the only cadet officially allowed to use a title, Lord Louis, later to become Earl Mountbatten of Burma.

OLD WINDSOR TO RICHMOND

Runnymede, Magna Carta and the Kennedy Memorial, ancient and more recent history combined in one place. The Charter that King John granted in these meadows on 15 June 1215 mentioned the removal of 'kiddles', derived from an old French word meaning 'a stake fence in a stream'. An even earlier Charter of King Richard I, dated 14 July 1197, commanded 'that all weirs that are in the Thames be removed'. The memorial to US President John F. Kennedy stands in an acre of land given to the USA by the British government.

Further downstream, a number of changes were made between the years 1930 and 1936 when vast works were undertaken. To cope with continual flooding, the Conservators instigated a series of works known as the Thames Improvement Scheme. This consisted of:

1) Building the Desborough channel below Shepperton lock.

2) Increasing the capacity of the weirs at Sunbury, Molesey and Teddington.

3) Widening and deepening the river between Shepperton and Teddington.

At the time it was estimated that over 1,000 hectares of land and 16 kilometres of roads would benefit from the scheme.

The Thames Conservancy No. 7 dredger in operation. Dredging operations often brought to the surface many interesting and sometimes valuable items such as Stone Age axe heads, Bronze Age spears, Viking swords and Roman coins. More recent items might include stone bottles, clay pipes, old Thames Conservancy licence plates and even firearms used in crimes and flung into the river to escape detection. What other secrets do the murky waters hold?

Looking upstream to Old Windsor lock before a major reconstruction programme in 1954. The brick-built lock was starting to show its age, and the decay can be seen near the lock access steps.

Old Windsor lock during remedial work in 1954, with nearly everything being replaced (apart from the house). This work must have caused severe disruption to river traffic and was no doubt noisy in the lock-house.

Salters steamer *Queen Elizabeth* passing through Old Windsor lock at the opening ceremony. The lock-house and the tree to its left appear to be the sole survivors of the rebuilding work. The grassy banks have been replaced by concrete steps, and while this may have saved on the lawn mowing, it is open to debate whether the overall appearance of the lock has been improved.

Town bridge, Windsor, suffering from the raging waters of the Thames in flood, 1947. A bridge has existed here for over 800 years, earlier ones being made of timber, while this cast-iron example was finally closed to vehicular traffic in about 1970.

Delivering the milk by punt at the junction of Oxford Road and Alma Road, Windsor, 1947. There were many such incidents in this most documented of Thames floods, including evacuations of stranded civilians by Army personnel.

Swan uppers photographed by Henry Taunt in Bell Weir lock, *c*. 1900. Swan upping was, and still is, a swan population census, carried out each July on the Thames. The swan was once a symbol of wealth, power and food and few were allowed to own them. Around 1275, when a goose was worth 5*d*, a swan was worth seven times as much. The penalties for killing, injuring or taking their eggs have always been severe; indeed one such villain was transported for seven years.

The Crown granted the privilege of ownership of a 'game' of swans to two London livery companies, the Dyers and the Vintners, and swan upping has been carried out since at least the fifteenth century. The cygnets are marked according to their parentage. Dyers' cygnets are marked with a single nick to the right side of the beak, and Vintners' have a nick on each side. Those belonging to the Crown remain unmarked. This ancient and colourful ceremony served a very useful purpose in recent years, when the uppers along with scientists from the Institute of Field Ornithology discovered a serious decline in the swan population. This was caused by lead poisoning from fishing weights, and the swan population has improved since with the introduction of weights made from other materials.

Manor ferry, situated about 1 km upstream from the Bells of Ousley pub, near Old Windsor. The fare for crossing was 6*d* for adults and 3*d* for under-twelves, dogs, prams and cycles. Ringing the bell seen here was necessary to gain the attention of the ferryman.

The Conservators' Centennial inspection of the London Stone at Staines, 1957. For about 600 years this stone marked the upper limit of jurisdiction of the Thames by the City of London. In 1857 the Thames Conservancy was formed and the City of London gave up all rights from Staines to the estuary. Among those attending the ceremony were Sir Jocelyn Bray (Chairman of the Conservators), Lord Glynn, Mr Joe Collett (Chief Navigation Inspector), and Mr H. Bowen (Lord Mayor of London). The Lord Mayor was fortunate in this case not to be bumped, a feature of past ceremonies!

The Penton Hook lock-keeper's daughter, Amy Kirby, exercising her ancient right of towing, while the family dog looks on. The flooding over the towpath below the lock caused more problems in the lock-house for the family, especially in the kitchen. When the river was very high the lock-keeper's wife had to put planks on bricks to avoid standing in floodwater while she was cooking!

Stephen Kirby, lock-keeper, at the tail of Penton Hook lock. On 11 April 1914 he heard cries for help and saw a boy being swept towards the weir after falling in the river. Without thought for his own safety, Mr Kirby jumped in and managed to save the boy from drowning. For his prompt and heroic action he was awarded two guineas, a medal and a certificate from the Thames Conservancy Board.

This beautiful and elaborately hand-painted Thames Conservancy certificate was awarded to Stephen Kirby for rescuing a drowning boy. The Thames Conservancy Board notified the Royal Humane Society about the incident and they too awarded a testimonial certificate.

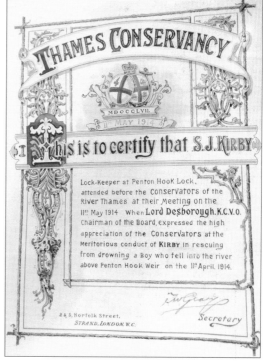

Removing or replacing the lock-gate at Chertsey lock, 1913. The sluices can be clearly seen at the bottom of the gate. At least twenty-four people were involved in this operation, not counting those who may be on the ropes out of the picture!

Chertsey weir, 1955. A disastrous collapse of the weir structure caused huge problems for the Thames Conservancy gang effecting repairs. Piles were driven in front of the buckled and twisted weir platform to dam off the water for repairs. Unusually, the entire flow of the Thames was diverted through Chertsey lock while work was carried out.

Salvaging a boat on Chertsey weir, 1955. The accident was a direct result of the collapse. It is unclear if the boat was swept through the weir, but showing clearly in the background are the remains of the weir platform.

Following the collapse of Chertsey weir, the Thames was diverted through the lock. In order to allow this, the lock-gates had to be winched open and then roped back. Unfortunately the ropes on one of the gates broke and the gate slammed shut. The increase in water pressure is obvious.

The floods of 1926. Believe it or not, underneath all this water lies Chertsey weir.

Aerial view of the Thames at Shepperton, where Docket Eddy Lane comes down to the river. Note the former course of the river delineated by the curved hedge in the centre of the photograph. According to Thames historian Fred Thacker, Docket Eddy is possibly a corruption of Dog Ait or Dock Ait, with the eddy most likely caused by the island (or ait).

Shepperton lock-house totally demolished by enemy action in 1940. The lock-keeper's wife and daughter both died in the attack, but the lock-keeper was absent at the time and survived.

Workmen clearing up the wreckage in the aftermath of the bombing at Shepperton lock.

Pack ice at Shepperton being broken up by the tug *Thames*, 1940.

The slipway and the distant Shepperton lock-house. This building served as the Thames Conservancy engineers' yard before the opening of the works at Sunbury. The large boat on the left is *Boy Jan*, and to the right of the slipway is the Dutch barge *Seven Bells*.

Increasing the width of the Thames below Shepperton lock, 1930s. The two workmen were building the retaining wall prior to the removal of the remainder of the bank on the left. Note the wooden profile boards for ensuring the wall is built correctly and the jackets hanging up on the earth bank!

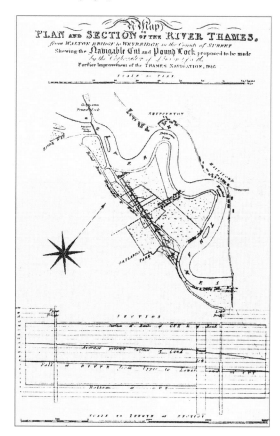

A copy of the 1812 City of London map, which proposed a pound lock cut on almost the same line as the scheme completed by the Thames Conservancy 123 years later.

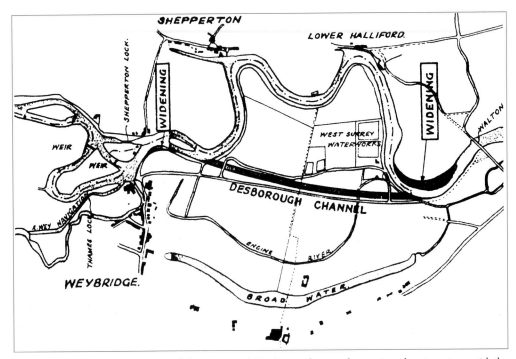

The Thames Conservancy map of the proposed Desborough cut, shortening the river to avoid the Shepperton and Halliford bends.

Cut along this line. The centreline of the Desborough cut is marked on this view of the water meadows between Walton and Weybridge, looking towards Weybridge before work started on the cut in the early 1930s.

The start of work on the Desborough cut, which immediately fills with water.

Aerial view looking downstream of work in progress on the Desborough cut. In the bottom left-hand corner is the old course of the river heading off to Shepperton and Halliford bends. It reappears at top left and heads off to Walton bridge, just visible in the distance. The road to the waterworks remains intact, while two new access bridges are being built.

Looking upstream towards Shepperton lock with work on the cut nearing completion.

The moment of truth for all the team involved with the Desborough cut – breaking through, with the usual number of interested onlookers.

Shortly after the channel was broken through, the steam launch *Donola* passed through. In the engine room was Mr Jack Reynolds, and at the bows waving his hat, Lord Desborough, no doubt pleased that his name would be forever associated with such a project.

One of the first vessels to pass downstream under the new bridges over the Desborough cut was the steamer *Viscount*.

The official opening of the Desborough cut, 10 July 1935.

The ramshackle shanty town just above Walton bridge, late 1930s. Compare this view to the permanent residences here today.

A Thames Conservancy diver at Coway Sale above Walton bridge, 1949. Possibly they are diving to examine the river bed for traces of the so-called 'Coway stakes', once thought to be remnants of the ancient crossing here. Curiously enough, just below Walton bridge is one of the deepest parts of the river.

Quite a few lads enjoying the fishing on Sunbury weir, in the days before rod licences and other restrictions prevented so many people from fishing on Thames weirs.

The vast quantities of flotsam and jetsam accumulated upon Sunbury weir overspill in 1970. It was often worse after Christmas when many Christmas trees were simply thrown into the river by people too lazy to dispose of them at the council tips. This led to many days' extra work for the lock-keeper cleaning the weir. Weir clearing was not only physically strenuous, but also potentially dangerous for the unwary.

Sunbury old lock. Although this lock is manually operated, it is often used during busy periods to clear the queues of boats. Occasionally boat-owners decide they are not going to wait for the lock-keeper's instructions and enter this lock on their own. On one occasion the summer assistant countered by padlocking the top gates shut! Such provocative behaviour is frowned upon, but it was successful in this instance and the offending vessel had to join the end of the queue of jeering boaters.

Looking downstream to the second Sunbury lock under construction, 1926. This lock-house was built in 1856 and eventually demolished in 1959. On the right, the white steps lead up to the old lock-house (just out of sight), built in 1812 and sometimes referred to as No. 1 lock-house. Built adjacent to the site of an earlier lock, this house (said to be haunted) was on three levels with accommodation for horses and bargees on the ground floor. Many cargoes were carried, including grain for Coxes mill on the River Wey. When the work was over, the horses were led over the cobbled bridge to graze on the island. According to Henry Taunt, there were trout-breeding ponds close to this house, of which no other evidence may be found.

Sunbury lock under construction, 1926. Confusion arose about the location of Sunbury lock in the 1950s, when an unwell boater died in the lock-house. Sunbury lock's location was in Walton-on-Thames, Surrey, but the telephone number was a Sunbury one, then in the county of Middlesex. The lock-keeper called for an ambulance and, while he waited, let a few boats through. Finding the access to Sunbury lock was difficult, with the address being in Walton and the dirt tracks to the lock easily missed. The dead boater meanwhile was laid on the kitchen floor of the lock-house, waiting. The agitated lock-keeper, not keen on his kitchen being a chapel of rest, called again. He was told the ambulance should have been with him a long time ago. More boats were let through. Eventually the ambulance arrived in a cloud of dust, and the body was removed on a stretcher. At the same time, a constable from Surrey police arrived on his bicycle. He told the ambulance crew in no uncertain terms that they could not take the body to Middlesex and that Surrey ambulance service must deal with it. An argument ensued. The angry Middlesex crew then unceremoniously rolled the body off the stretcher on to the lockside and promptly left. Muttering under his breath about a report, the policeman also departed. With the poor fellow face down on the lock side and a gathering crowd of onlookers and more boats waiting to be let through, the lock-keeper and his assistant decided to carry the body off to the old lock office. Once inside he was sat upright and locked in. Perhaps they thought he would be safer that way. Resisting the urge to check on the dear departed, the lock-keeper carried on letting boats through. The correct crew from Surrey eventually arrived and the (very) late boater made his final journey by road.

The steam tug *Ham* in the second lock at Sunbury on 24 January 1927, shortly after the official opening. The old lock, built in 1856 and still used today during busy periods, may be seen to the left of the picture.

The Magpie Hotel, Lower Sunbury, 1890s. It was owned by Thomas Freeman and his father before him, and father and son are standing on the steps at the back of the hotel. The boat in the foreground was built by Emm's boat builders of Kingston. Almost 14 m long, steam-powered and capable of carrying twelve passengers, this elegant craft was probably owned by Salters Steamers. It is unclear why this boat should be in the Sunbury backwater.

The largest private motor yacht on the Thames, *Dahu*, passing Tagg's island and hotel, 1958. Owned by Mr Roydhouse, this yacht was over 30 m long and was intended to be taken to Cornwall. Having failed a survey it ended up at Windsor Sea Cadets, where the vessel suffered neglect until it was bought and immaculately restored for a vintage rally in France.

Coracle racing outside Tom Tagg's boatyard. The early coracles were made of willow twigs (withies) covered with animal hides. More recent versions, however, have wooden laths and treated canvas. Tom Tagg was considered to be one of the finest boat-builders of the time. His family origins can be traced back to Holland, where the family name was Taag. This was considered to be too difficult for the English tongue to master and consequently changed.

Molesey weir being upgraded in 1932, with steel gates being lowered into place. This work was carried out to improve control over the lower reaches of the Thames and minimize flooding .

A poor-quality picture of Molesey lock, included because of the second lock visible to the left of the picture. Thought to exist for only a year, and mentioned in the Conservators' minutes of 1913, the extra lock was needed for the huge volume of coal bound for Hampton Wharf.

The lock-keeper and permanent assistant, Mr John Jeffrey, ice breaking in Molesey lock, 2 February 1954.

Looking down from the tail of Molesey lock, 1906, shortly after the lock was rebuilt. In the background is the earlier Hampton Court bridge, replaced by the present one in 1933/4. Note the number of punts, onlookers, a photographer and the steamer on the right-hand bank.

The house boat *Irene* sank just below Molesey lock, 29 March 1933. Note the loaded barge waiting to go through the lock. The volume of barge traffic through Molesey lock was so great that another temporary lock was constructed on the upstream side of the rollers.

The replacement Hampton Court bridge under construction, *c*. 1933, looking upstream to Molesey lock and weir. Below the new bridge can be seen extensive widening and dredging of the main channel and the start of bank re-profiling.

A view of the two bridges at Hampton Court and the Palace, *c.* 1934. In this view note the re-profiled river bank nearing completion and the River Mole joining the Thames.

Dismantling of the old Hampton Court bridge, *c.* 1934. With the new bridge open to traffic, taking down the huge cast-iron cylinders that were the main supports for the bridge proved to be quite a task.

Kingston had a bad year in 1928, with barges sinking and the fire at Gridley Miskins yard (see below). Here, timber barges are jammed on to the bridge, looking from the Surrey side and downstream.

The fire at Gridley Miskins timber yard, Kingston, 11 August 1928. The fire was so fierce that it burnt for three days and nights. It is amazing that people would want to position themselves so close to potential danger.

The severely damaged wreck of a tug on Teddington weir. This must have been quite a frightening experience for the crew. If the tug remained here too long, the build-up of water pressure on the hull could break the tug up completely and sink it, so it was essential for salvage crews to act swiftly to clear the weir.

'Coal mining' at Teddington, 18 December 1930. This rather atmospheric photograph was actually the commencement of work to increase the capacity of Teddington weir. As part of the Thames Improvement Scheme, new sluices were installed here and at Molesey and Sunbury. Never underestimate the power of nature: accumulated ice burst weirs here in 1827 and again fifty years later.

The official opening by Lord Desborough of the new sluices at Teddington weir in 1932. There were a total of five lock-keepers at Teddington to cope with the twenty-four hour running of the lock. The No. 1 lock-keeper had the privilege of wearing three buttons on his sleeve as seen here.

Flooding at Teddington lock in 1928, with a launch wreck at the entrance to the 'coffin' or skiff lock. This tiny lock remains something of a curiosity being only 1.77 m wide and hand operated by a peculiar levered sluice arrangement.

The boundary stone below Teddington lock, 1929, marking the start of the jurisdiction of the Port of London Authority over the River Thames.

Richmond weir and footbridge, 1906. It was officially opened on 19 May 1894 by HRH the Duke of York. After thirty years of argument, Parliament gave assent to the grandly titled 'The Richmond Sluice, Lock and Slipway Bill' and work commenced in about 1890. Some detailed changes to the original design presented to Parliament were made before work started. The width of the lock was increased along two-thirds of its length to accommodate extra barges. Also, instead of the original seven arches with spans of 12 m, the spans were increased to 20 m, making the five arches seen here. The three central arches of the bridge contained counter-balanced sluices that were lowered on a falling tide to maintain the water level around half-tide mark. On the Twickenham side boat rollers are just visible, while the 'half tide' lock is on the opposite bank. When the sluices were opened, vessels passed through them on tidal water; at other times they had to pass through the lock and pay a toll. In 1909 the Port of London Authority took over control of the lock from the Thames Conservancy.

ACKNOWLEDGEMENTS

I am very pleased to be able to acknowledge the help of everyone who offered information and lent photographs for this book; apologies to anyone I may have omitted. While every effort has been made to trace the copyright owners or the photographers, some errors may have occurred. If this is the case, corrections will be made in later editions. Bert Batiste, Joan Barfoot, Ken Berg, Reg Bolland, Paul Brenchley, Jim Brown, Harry Brunnock, Glynis Carroll, Elizabeth Chaplin, Peter Chaplin, John Chittenden, Tom Christie, Ken Clarke, Peter Clarke, Joe Collett, Dave Crombie, Darrell Cruickshank, Arthur Cushing, Mike Davies, Nigel Dawe, Melanie Delve, Phyllis Dudman, 'Fishy' Jack Eade, Sylvia Eade, George Fielder, Jim Goodall, Darran Gough, Dick Greenaway, Joyce Griffin, Chris Groves, Simon Hills, Stan Holland, Mr Hunnon, John Jeffrey, John King, Kenny Knight, Philip Kirby, Walter Kyte, Robin Laurence, Michael Lancashire, Edward Leach, Emily Leach, Ron Lloyd, Bill Mcreadie, Don Mackaskill, Steve Newman, Robin Newlands, Len Overy, Graham Parlour, Steve Pickford, Laurence Poole, Thomas Poore, John Powell, Rowland Raynor, Peter Rowe, Marion Rees, Eleanor Simpson, Paul Sims, Joey Sims, Pauline Smith, Fred Smith, David Thacker, D. Mckintyre-Ure, Mark Vinden, Keith Webb, Bob Williams, David Wilson, E.A. Wilson, Fred Windsor, Tony Wright.

Aerial Photo Company, Associated Newspapers, Central Press Photos, Colourbox Techunique, Collier & Guy Press Photographers, Great Western Railways, Goring and Streatley Local History Society, Leading Edge Computers, National Rivers Authority, *North Berks Herald*, Oxford Photocrafts, Planet News, RCHME, Reading Museum, Richmond Local History Society, River and Rowing Museum.

I am also grateful to the late Elspeth Huxley for permission to use an amended quote from *The Flame Trees of Thika* in the introduction.

During the compilation of this book I have consulted many excellent works for information. Unfortunately because of space restrictions I am unable to provide a bibliography but I hope this book has whetted your appetite to seek them out for yourselves.

BRITAIN IN OLD PHOTOGRAPHS

Lincoln
Lincoln Cathedral
The Lincolnshire Coast
Liverpool
Around Llandudno
Around Lochaber
Theatrical London
Around Louth
The Lower Fal Estuary
Lowestoft
Luton
Lympne Airfield
Lytham St Annes
Maidenhead
Around Maidenhead
Around Malvern
Manchester
Manchester Road & Rail
Mansfield
Marlborough: A Second Selection
Marylebone & Paddington
Around Matlock
Melton Mowbray
Around Melksham
The Mendips
Merton & Morden
Middlesbrough
Midsomer Norton & Radstock
Around Mildenhall
Milton Keynes
Minehead
Monmouth & the River Wye
The Nadder Valley
Newark
Around Newark
Newbury
Newport, Isle of Wight
The Norfolk Broads
Norfolk at War
North Fylde
North Lambeth
North Walsham & District
Northallerton
Northampton
Around Norwich
Nottingham 1944–74
The Changing Face of Nottingham
Victorian Nottingham
Nottingham Yesterday & Today
Nuneaton
Around Oakham
Ormskirk & District
Otley & District
Oxford: The University
Oxford Yesterday & Today
Oxfordshire Railways: A Second
  Selection
Oxfordshire at School
Around Padstow
Pattingham & Wombourne

Penwith
Penzance & Newlyn
Around Pershore
Around Plymouth
Poole
Portsmouth
Poulton-le-Fylde
Preston
Prestwich
Pudsey
Radcliffe
RAF Chivenor
RAF Cosford
RAF Hawkinge
RAF Manston
RAF Manston: A Second Selection
RAF St Mawgan
RAF Tangmere
Ramsgate & Thanet Life
Reading
Reading: A Second Selection
Redditch & the Needle District
Redditch: A Second Selection
Richmond, Surrey
Rickmansworth
Around Ripley
The River Soar
Romney Marsh
Romney Marsh: A Second
  Selection
Rossendale
Around Rotherham
Rugby
Around Rugeley
Ruislip
Around Ryde
St Albans
St Andrews
Salford
Salisbury
Salisbury: A Second Selection
Salisbury: A Third Selection
Around Salisbury
Sandhurst & Crowthorne
Sandown & Shanklin
Sandwich
Scarborough
Scunthorpe
Seaton, Lyme Regis & Axminster
Around Seaton & Sidmouth
Sedgley & District
The Severn Vale
Sherwood Forest
Shrewsbury
Shrewsbury: A Second Selection
Shropshire Railways
Skegness
Around Skegness
Skipton & the Dales
Around Slough

Smethwick
Somerton & Langport
Southampton
Southend-on-Sea
Southport
Southwark
Southwell
Southwold to Aldeburgh
Stafford
Around Stafford
Staffordshire Railways
Around Staveley
Stepney
Stevenage
The History of Stilton Cheese
Stoke-on-Trent
Stoke Newington
Stonehouse to Painswick
Around Stony Stratford
Around Stony Stratford: A Second
  Selection
Stowmarket
Streatham
Stroud & the Five Valleys
Stroud & the Five Valleys: A
  Second Selection
Stroud's Golden Valley
The Stroudwater and Thames &
  Severn Canals
The Stroudwater and Thames &
  Severn Canals: A Second
  Selection
Suffolk at Work
Suffolk at Work: A Second
  Selection
The Heart of Suffolk
Sunderland
Sutton
Swansea
Swindon: A Third Selection
Swindon: A Fifth Selection
Around Tamworth
Taunton
Around Taunton
Teesdale
Teesdale: A Second Selection
Tenbury Wells
Around Tettenhall & Codshall
Tewkesbury & the Vale of
  Gloucester
Thame to Watlington
Around Thatcham
Around Thirsk
Thornbury to Berkeley
Tipton
Around Tonbridge
Trowbridge
Around Truro
TT Races
Tunbridge Wells

Tunbridge Wells: A Second
  Selection
Twickenham
Uley, Dursley & Cam
The Upper Fal
The Upper Tywi Valley
Uxbridge, Hillingdon & Cowley
The Vale of Belvoir
The Vale of Conway
Ventnor
Wakefield
Wallingford
Walsall
Waltham Abbey
Wandsworth at War
Wantage, Faringdon & the Vale
  Villages
Around Warwick
Weardale
Weardale: A Second Selection
Wednesbury
Wells
Welshpool
West Bromwich
West Wight
Weston-super-Mare
Around Weston-super-Mare
Weymouth & Portland
Around Wheatley
Around Whetstone
Whitchurch to Market Drayton
Around Whitstable
Wigton & the Solway Plain
Willesden
Around Wilton
Wimbledon
Around Windsor
Wingham, Addisham &
  Littlebourne
Wisbech
Witham & District
Witney
Around Witney
The Witney District
Wokingham
Around Woodbridge
Around Woodstock
Woolwich
Woolwich Royal Arsenal
Around Wootton Bassett,
  Cricklade & Purton
Worcester
Worcester in a Day
Around Worcester
Worcestershire at Work
Around Worthing
Wotton-under-Edge to Chipping
  Sodbury
Wymondham & Attleborough
The Yorkshire Wolds